The Food of Southern Italy and Calabria

From the mountains to the sea,
recipes for the soul

by
Francesco Altomare

Copyright © 2015 Francesco Altomare

All rights reserved, including the right to reproduce this book, or portions thereof in any form. No part of this text may be reproduced, transmitted, downloaded, decompiled, reverse engineered, or stored, in any form or introduced into any information storage and retrieval system, in any form or by any means, whether electronic or mechanical without the express written permission of the author.

The views expressed in this work are solely those of the author and do not necessarily reflect the views of the publisher, and the publisher hereby disclaims any responsibility for them.

ISBN: 978-1-326-50322-2

PublishNation
www.publishnation.co.uk

Introduction

Cucina povera

I am stumbling through a lemon grove on the steep slopes of Mount Vesuvius looking for somewhere cool to sit under the shade of a tree. The scent of the lemons, fill me with joy and in the morning's misty distance I can see the bay of Naples. The sky and sea are a dazzling blue as I take out a panini which I bought earlier from an old lady in a shop in 'Torre del Greco'; a small grimy town on the footsteps of Vesuvius. The filling is layers of mozzarella cheese and grilled aubergine. I savour every mouthful whilst contemplating how a Royal Navy sailor ends up living and working in this manic, sleazy, edgy, but beautiful city that is Naples. As a bonus I live within driving distance of my ancestral Calabria so I get to eat some of the best food in the world; 'cucina povera'.

That was over thirty-five years ago and cucina povera was almost unknown outside southern Italy. Today cucina povera is regaled and served in some of the most expensive restaurants around the world.

How bemused the people who lived 'cucina povera' out of necessity would be to see that.

South of Naples is a land of brooding hills, mountains, forests, lakes, and a coastline of crystalline sea. Villages cling precariously to the side of mountains. In these villages are a proud, tough, resilient people. They are shaped by landscape, invasion, community, family, tradition and migration. These are a people of great generosity of spirit. They are the creators of cucina povera.

When I look back over the years I realise just how lucky I was, and how a lifetime's interest in the food of Southern Italy started. As a child I would watch my Mum prepare simple but flavoursome food that my school friends could only dream of; a woman that had been given a gift by god when it came to cooking, my inspiration comes from her. Even today I cannot recreate the wonderful Ragu sauce she made but I am getting close. The recipes in this book are a tribute to her and the wonderful people of Southern Italy who passed on their knowledge with generosity, enthusiasm and love. These are the people that cucina povera are all about.

The recipes in this book are a collection of memories from the past and the present. They are only intended as a 'guide' because cucina povera is itself dependent on what you have. All the recipes have been tried and tested and are open to mild tweaking depending on what is in your store.

Frank Altomare

Zuppa de pesilli e pattate

Pea and potato soup

A winter afternoon in the Calabrian highlands

The village of Rogliano in the highlands of Calabria sits serenely some 660 metres above sea level surrounded by the chestnut covered Southern Apennines. It is a typical mountain village of Southern Italy. Stone houses with terracotta roofs huddle close together along steep roads barely wide for one car to pass. There is no Bougainvillea as there is in towns on the coast; the winters here are hard and cold. Logs are collected during the hot summer months to be used in the fire places during the cold months of winter and are stored in huge piles in back gardens.

The tradition of preserving food is still practiced widely. Air dried ham, capocollo, and salami hang in cellars and outhouses. Sundried figs, porcini mushrooms, dried peas, and bottled tomatoes are stored away for use later in the year.

The recipe below was cooked by my uncle one winter afternoon at his farm just outside the village, around us the hills were capped with snow; he used dried peas which had been soaked in salted water the night before. We sat eating the soup in the stone walled kitchen with the smell of wood smoke wafting from the fire. It's the simple things that bring the greatest pleasure.

Ingredients for 4

Two mugs of frozen or fresh peas,
or dried (soaked overnight and drained)

One medium potato

One medium onion

Two peeled garlic cloves

Pinch of chilli flakes to taste

750ml of chicken stock, or one stock cube in 750ml of water.

Method

Preheat oven to 180C

Take the onion and peel, and chop onion into quarters.

Take the garlic cloves and place on a baking dish along with the quartered onions, and drizzle with olive oil. Place in to oven and roast till brown.

In the meantime peel and dice the potato.

Remove the onions and garlic when they are brown from oven, and place to one side.

In a heavy bottomed sauce pan add a generous glug of olive oil.

Place on heat and add the diced potatoes and fry over a gentle heat then add the onions and the garlic and stir gently for a few minutes.

Add the peas and the stock and bring to a simmer for 15 minutes, then add chilli and blitz with a blender until smooth. For a more rustic soup do not blitz. At this point the soup might be quite thick and you may wish to add more stock to increase the amount of soup. Add salt and pepper to taste and serve with crusty bread. As a variation grate pecorino cheese on to the soup before serving.

Calamari

I first tasted calamari in Naples in 1978. It was in a restaurant near Poslillipo, Naples. The restaurant was nestled by the water with colourful fishing boats moored nearby, and where equally colourful language could be heard from the fisherman. Being a seafood restaurant in Naples we were going to be in for a treat.

There are many ways to cook calamari or fried squid rings. Some like to cook them coated in bread crumbs or in a light batter. I prefer to cook them very simply dusted is seasoned fine semolina flour.

Ingredients for 2

One whole medium sized squid from a fishmonger

One teacup of plain semolina flour

Salt and pepper

Lemon wedges to serve.

Method

You can ask the fishmonger to clean the squid and skin it for you. If preparing yourself then take the squid to the sink and pull the head, (the part with the tentacles) away from the body. Inside the body reach in with your fingers and pull out the thin transparent cartilage and dispose of it. Turn the body inside out and rinse under running water removing any gunk. Turn the body the right way round and with a sharp knife make a small nick in the skin and with your fingers remove this outer skin. Place the cleaned squid (tube) on to a board and cut into rings about 8mm wide. Take the head of the squid and remove the tentacles and discard the rest.

In a deep saucepan add plenty of cooking oil so as to deep fry the calamari. Place on the heat and keep a careful eye on it. In a plastic container with a lid place the squid rings and the tentacles. Then add the seasoned flour, place the lid back on and shake to coat the squid evenly. When the oil is hot take handful of the squid and shake off any surplus flour.

Drop the dusted squid carefully into the hot oil and as soon as the calamari have turned golden remove from the oil and place on to kitchen paper to drain continue until all the squid are cooked. Serve immediately with a crispy salad and wedges of lemon.

Fiori di zucchini

Courgette flowers

In the village markets of southern Italy one can see sacks of these flowers for sale. I think I am in love with these bright yellow flowers; I would eat them all day long if I could. Fried in a light batter they are a crunchy and full of flavour. They are so easy to prepare, the most difficult thing is getting the flowers, not a problem if you grow courgettes.. They should be picked first thing in the morning just before they have had time to open.

Ingredients

Courgette flowers

Plain flour

Sparkling water

Salt and pepper to taste

Variation (Ricotta cheese)

Sunflower oil to fry

Method

Heat the oil in a deep fryer to a temperature that you would fry chips at. Alternatively, I use a saucepan and I keep a close eye on it and drop a bit of batter into the oil to see if it is hot enough.

You need to make a batter from plain flour which has been very well seasoned with salt and pepper. To this flour add freezing cold sparkling water. Whisk the batter until it is smooth and without lumps. It should not be too thick; it should just coat the flowers with a fine veil.

After you have washed each courgette flower, take it by the stem and dip it into the batter and shake off any drips. Place gently and carefully into the hot oil. You will need to turn them over as they will float on the surface of the oil. As soon as the batter coated flowers have turned golden on both sides lift them out to drain on kitchen paper and serve immediately.

A variation to this would be to stuff the inside of the flower with seasoned ricotta cheese before dipping into the batter and then straight into the hot oil.

MELENZANE SOTTO OLIO

GRILLED AUBERGINE IN OLIVE OIL

Ingredients for 4

1-2 aubergine(s)

¼ of a small, medium hot chilli pepper chopped finely

Small hand full of fresh mint leaves

1 clove of garlic finely chopped

¼ cup of olive oil

Salt and pepper

Method

Place a griddle pan on the hob to pre-heat to full heat setting.

Slice the aubergine length wise into slices of about 6-8mm wide. Place in a deep dish and drizzle well with some olive oil.

Place the aubergine slices onto the griddle and cook on one side for 2-3 minutes or until charred griddle lines are well developed, then turn the slices over and repeat.

Remove from griddle and place on kitchen paper to cool.

When cool place the sliced griddled aubergine into a medium deep serving dish.

Add the olive oil into the dish, sprinkle on the chopped chilli, and sprinkle on the chopped garlic and the mint leaves, ensure that all the aubergines are evenly covered.

Allow the dish to marinate for at least a few hours or better still overnight.

Serve with warm crusty bread.

ZUCCINI AL FERRO CON ALIO E OLIO

Grilled courgettes with olive oil and garlic

Courgettes, Cousin Gaetano, a Fiat 500, 1970, and the beach at Falerno, Calabria

My cousin Gaetano is already up and waiting with my Uncle Gigi in an old dark blue Fiat 500I'm late and they'll leave without me. 'Are you coming?' shouts my Uncle; 'Si!' I reply while pulling on my jeans. It's 8am and the sun is already hot. My cousin and I run up the hill while our uncles get into the car and drive it to the top of the hill and wait for us. This performance is needed as the little Fiat can't make it up the hill with all four of us in it. Once in the car we're off; my Uncle driving like he'd just stolen it, we wind our way crazily down out of the village and on to the motorway. Fifty short but death defying minutes later we arrive at Falerno, and the beach. Uncle Frank paves the way across the hot sand to the water's edge. For some reason he always finds a place near to some bikini clad young ladies. The uncles spend the rest of the morning looking at and flirting with the girls, while Gaetano and I spend so much time in the warm blue water that we come out like wrinkled old men. Lunch time arrives, the ladies are forgotten, and a BBQ is made up of a ring of large stones and drift wood. Out comes the bread, lamb cutlets, and courgettes, lunch is prepared.

The courgettes seared on the metal grill were the star of this simple beach lunch.

Ingredients for 2

2 medium courgettes

1 medium garlic clove

Balsamic vinegar

Olive oil

Four mint leaves to taste

Salt and pepper

Preparation

Pre-heat a griddle pan to maximum heat. Slice courgettes into thin slices roughly 5mm thick along the length of the courgette, place in a shallow bowl and drizzle with a little olive oil. Layer the sliced courgettes on to the hot griddle pan. Do not overcrowd courgettes in the pan. After a few minutes the courgettes should be char grilled on one side, turn over and repeat process. When cooked evenly remove from pan and place back in shallow bowl. Continue until all the slices are cooked and char grilled on both sides.

Slice the garlic clove very thinly and toss on to the courgettes cooling in the bowl, tossing them in while the courgettes are still cooling. Once the courgettes are cool, drizzle with olive oil, and good quality balsamic vinegar. Chop up four mint leaves and add to the bowl. Add salt and pepper to taste and stir the contents of the bowl well. This recipe works really well on a BBQ, or on the beach and bikinis are optional.

Pasta fatta a casa

Homemade Pasta

The majority of pasta eaten in Italy tends to be dry shop brought. There are many reasons for this. The two main reasons are time, and the quality of shop bought pasta, which is very good.

However I think homemade pasta tends to be better. I don't often make homemade pasta, but when I do it is always very satisfying in all sorts of ways. You don't need much in the way of equipment although you can buy a pasta making machine. You will still need to make the dough by hand but you can use the machine to roll the sheets.

Ingredients

6 eggs

About 600 grams of plain flour, type 00 or strong bread making flour.

Method

Pour the flour into a heap on your work surface and with your hand make a hollow in the centre of the mound for the eggs. Add the eggs to the centre and with a fork gently stir the eggs together. Then with your hands bring the flour into the egg mix. When the eggs have absorbed as much flour as they can it will be time to start kneading the dough. Continue to knead the dough until it is smooth and moist. You may need to add more flour to get the right consistency. When kneading it is worth using the bottom half of your palm and turning the dough as you go.

You are now ready to roll the pasta dough; you can do this by hand or use your machine to do this. The machine will have a set of rollers which you can adjust step by step to get the pasta to the right thickness for your needs. For Lasagne No5 and for Linguine No6, but it is all down to personal preference.

Remember that homemade linguine pasta cooks very quickly. Place it into boiling salted water and as soon as it rises to the surface remove from the water and serve with the sauce of your choice.

Semolina pasta

As a variation pasta can be made without eggs using only fine semolina flour and water. Personally I prefer this type of pasta. You can also make this pasta in a pasta extruding machine.

Ingredients

300 grams of fine semolina flour

Half to one full cup of water

Method

Place the semolina flour into a bowl then add water a little at a time (about a tablespoon at a time) whilst combining the mixture together. You need fairly stiff dough, knead for about 10 minutes or so. Place the dough in cling wrap and rest in the fridge for half an hour. After this time you can create your own pasta shapes by rolling out thinly on a floured surface, cutting and shaping as you wish.

You can make simple bow tie shapes, Oreccihiette, and many more. YouTube carries endless shapes that you can make with this recipe. Enjoy.

Note that if you are using a pasta extruder attachment (highly recommended) you will need to make the pasta following the instructions that come with the machine as otherwise it will be too soft and sticky to extrude.

Tomato ragu sauce for pasta

This recipe is the basis for all the (heavy) tomato sauces, as opposed to the light fresh tomatoes used in the other recipes. The sauce is also used for lasagne, some pizza topping, and for the slow cooking of meats in tomato sauce. It is cooked for a long time; up to four hours is not uncommon. Use a heavy bottomed sauce pan so the heat is distributed evenly. Keep an eye on the pan as you won't want the sauce to scorch. If you are adding meat to this sauce make sure to brown the meat first.

Ingredients

Two tins of good quality tomatoes or twelve fresh peeled chopped plum tomatoes

2 tablespoons of tomato concentrate

Water as needed

Olive oil

One or two garlic cloves

Bay leaf (optional)

One glass of red wine (optional)

Salt and pepper to taste

Method

In a heavy bottomed saucepan add 3-4 tablespoons of olive oil, place on a low heat and add the garlic cloves and heat them gently but do not brown. If using meat add at this stage and brown. Add the two tins of tomatoes or the fresh tomatoes and then add the same amount of water bring to a boil and then lower to a simmer. Now add the tomato concentrate and stir in. Add the bay leaf and the wine. Continue cooking on a simmer and place a loose lid over the saucepan. Simmer for at least two hours adding more water as necessary (you are looking to achieve a thick dark sauce, about two thirds the amount of the two tins of tomatoes).

Any meat, or meat balls will by now have become tender and succulent, continue to simmer gently until you are happy to serve.

Pasta aglio e olio

Olive oil and garlic pasta

When the dark leaden skies are only matched by your mood and it's been a rotten day, you're tired, you've finished work late and there's nothing in the cupboard to eat, you really don't want to go shopping, and it's started to rain. Well this is where aglio e olio pasta comes to the rescue; it will bring some sunshine and the warm scented breeze of the Mediterranean in to your home. It is the quickest dish you will ever make and is wonderfully tasty to boot. In Italy it is sometimes called 'pasta di mezzanotte' or 'midnight pasta' for when you return home late and hunger pangs strike. You really need only olive oil, garlic and spaghetti to make this, if you have the rest of the ingredients then it will be even better.

Ingredients for 2

200 grams of spaghetti

4 tablespoons of olive oil

1 or 2 garlic cloves finely chopped

Chilli flakes to taste (optional)

Breadcrumbs (optional)

Chopped flat leaf parsley (optional)

Salt and pepper to taste

Method

Place a large pan of salted water onto boil. Add the olive oil, garlic and chilli flakes to a frying pan and heat gently. Do not brown the garlic, but cook until soft. Then raise the temperature of the frying pan and add the breadcrumbs and fry till crispy and golden. By now the spaghetti will be cooked, drain the pasta and add directly to the frying pan mixing it all well. If it looks dry add some water from the pan you cooked the pasta in. Sprinkle on the parsley and stir. Serve immediately

An old shepherd, Albanian villages, pasta and pecorino cheese

'La Sila' in Calabria is one of the last alpine areas of southern Europe, most if not all, is national park. The park is split into three different areas: Grand Sila, Small Sila, and the Greek Sila. With an average height of 1200mts above sea level, La Sila has much to offer, alpine pastures, huge pines, lakes, and wonderful cheeses and salumi. The wolf, eagle owl, flora and fauna are some of its many attractions. In winter deep snow covers the area and in summer La Sila provides a welcome respite from the heat of the coast. It was here in la Sila that I chanced upon a biblical scene of a shepherd tending his sheep. This shepherd led a simple life but he seemed rich in inner contentment. There must be something very special about coming to a point in life when you realise that we all tend to complicate our lives with what we think is important and desirable. Often these important and desirable things are only that when we first get them, after a while you find that they are not the things that first appeared so essential to have.

I stopped to watch him and we fell into conversation. He talked about how the young no longer wanted the life of a shepherd and only a very few of the new Albanians emigrants would work as shepherds. I asked if he and the Albanians could understand each other. 'We can, and we can't, we speak in a similar tongue' he replied, 'but it is difficult to understand these new Albanians in so many ways, I'm not sure about them at all', he said. It was then that the penny dropped, the shepherd was from one of the old Italo-Albanian villages in la Sila which have existed since the mid fourteen hundreds. These Albanian villages came into being hundreds of years ago as Christian Albanians escaped the Turkish invasions. They found peace and sanctuary in the Calabrian highlands and the descendants still speak an ancient Albanian today. We chatted on about his life and the food that they eat. He told me about how they make the best pecorino cheese in Italy (everyone in Italy thinks they make the best pecorino), of homemade pasta, and simple food that he enjoyed. After a short while we both had to move on, but before leaving he told me where I could buy pecorino cheese that was the best in the area. I followed his directions to a small store and bought half a round of a small cheese. The cheese was very good! I think that the following recipe goes so well with this cheese.

Courgette, mint and pecorino cheese pasta

Ingredients for 2

One medium courgette

Five shredded mint leaves

Cup full of grated pecorino cheese

250 grams of pasta conchiglie no 50 or penne, or even homemade pasta

Two tablespoons of olive oil

Method

Place a large pan of salted water on to boil.

In the meantime cut the courgette into small cubes and add to a large frying pan with the olive oil and cook gently. Turn up the heat on the frying pan as the pan of salted water comes to the boil. Add a ladle of the boiling water to the frying pan. Add the pasta to the boiling water. When the courgette becomes soft, mash them to a pulp with a fork or potato masher, turn the heat to low, and add the shredded mint leaves.

When the pasta has almost cooked remove a large mug of the water and reserve, drain the pasta and tip it into the frying pan with the courgette pulp. Turn the heat up to medium and add the grated pecorino and mix together. At this point if the dish looks a little dry add a little of the reserved water in which the pasta was boiled. Serve straight away.

Courgette and ricotta pasta

The simple courgette is transformed into a mouth-watering dish in this simple cheap and healthy recipe. I would encourage you to cook this dish as it is so easy and so tasty. This recipe should serve 4 people. This recipe goes well with homemade pasta but is almost as good with shop bought dry pasta.

Ingredients

2 tablespoons of Olive oil

2 to 3 courgettes

Small tub of ricotta

Chopped flat leaf parsley

Salt and pepper to taste

500 grms of spaghetti or linguine

Grated parmesan cheese

Method

Place a large pan of salted water onto boil for the pasta. Cut eatch courgettes in to four lengths and then chop the lengths up into segments about 3-4mm width. In a large frying pan add about 3-4 tablespoons of olive oil and heat gently. Add the chopped courgettes and fry gently until soft, do not allow the courgettes to brown. Place the spaghetti on to cook when the water is boiling. When the pasta is 3 mins from being cooked, turn out the ricotta into the frying pan with the courgettes and mix well. Add plenty of ground black pepper and salt to taste. Drain the pasta and reserve some of the water. Place the drained pasta into the frying pan and mix together well and add the chopped parsley. Now add about 2 tablespoons of the grated parmesan and mix again. At this stage you may well find that the dish looks a little dry. Take the reserved water and ladle some into the mix until you have a nice loose sauce. Serve straight away.

PASTA GAMBARI

Fresh tomato and prawn pasta

The Port of Sapri in Campania

The small port of Sapri is the last, or the first coastal town of Campania depending on weather you are traveling north or south on the SS18 coastal road. It sits in a perfect little bay between two National Parks, Pollino to the south and Cliento to the north. It's not a particularly attractive town, the seafront being its best asset. But at the end of the town there is a small port to the south of the bay which is shared by swanky looking yachts and the far more interesting grubby fishing boats consigned to the far end of the port. Here you can find all manner of the fruits of the sea. You need to be up early at the port, six am is not too early. The colourful fishing boats deliver their catch on to the harbour side where refrigerated vans wait. Octopus, squid, sea bream, live prawns, clams, and sometimes huge tuna and swordfish glisten in the morning sunshine. In the early morning air the smells of fresh fish, nets drying, seaweed, and fuel oil all mingle together, I think it's an experience not to miss. It was here that I bought some raw prawns.

I know it's not easy to get hold of fresh raw prawns, but if you can then you will be in for an even bigger treat. Please don't use the ridiculously expensive raw king prawns that have been farmed somewhere in Indonesia. The small British shell on prawn is cheaper and far better for this recipe.

Fresh tomato and prawn pasta

Ingredients for 4

3 tablespoons of olive oil

1 glass of white wine (optional)

¼ of a small, medium hot chilli pepper chopped finely.

Wand of parsley

Small handful of chopped parsley

12 small cherry tomatoes cut in half

1 small red onion finely chopped

1 clove of garlic finely chopped

500-600 grams shell on prawns

If using shelled prawns, peel the prawns first, and keep heads to one side

500 grams of dry spaghetti

Handful of fresh parsley finely chopped

Salt and pepper

Method

Place a large pan of salted water on the hob to boil, when the water is boiling add the spaghetti.

In a medium frying pan add the olive oil, the parsley wand, the sliced garlic and for extra flavour if you prefer, the heads of the prawns along with the white wine. Fry gently over a low heat pressing the juices from the prawn heads with a wooden spoon. After five or so minutes decant the contents of the frying pan into a strainer and extract the resultant liquid back into the frying pan, you can aid this along by using a wooden spoon to force out the liquid. Then add the onions to the pan and fry gently till translucent. Then add the cut tomatoes, gently squeeze them over the pan before dropping them in so as to release the juice). Cook on a medium heat for one minute before adding the fresh peeled prawns. Turn up the heat and add the chilli flakes and salt to taste, and continue to cook until prawns are heated through.

By now the pasta should be cooked, drain the pasta reserving the cooking water. Add the chopped parsley to the frying pan and stir. Turn down the heat to low and add the drained spaghetti to the frying pan and toss until all the spaghetti is coated. If the pasta looks a little dry add some of the reserved water.

Transfer to warmed bowls and serve.

Pasta Vongole

Pasta with clams

This recipe is very popular all over Italy and is varied in which ever region it is being cooked in. I think that this dish is stunning; it is one of my favourites. If you are near the beaches around the East coast of England then you can dig for your own cockles and use them instead, I did this a few years ago and it was a revelation. Whatever you use please make sure that you wash and scrub them well. You don't want sand in your pasta vongole. This dish is best served with spaghetti or linguine.

Ingredients

For two

Olive oil

Parsley stem

Clove of garlic

1 glass of dry white wine

600grm of live clams

Chopped parsley

Salt and pepper to taste

Optional chilli flakes to taste

Method

Place a large pan of salted water on the heat to boil, when the water is boiling add your spaghetti.

To a large shallow pan add about 3 tablespoons of olive oil, place pan on a gentle heat and add the stem of parsley, chilli flakes and the peeled garlic clove. Continue to heat the pan gently until the garlic has softened slightly. At this point remove the garlic and the stem from the pan and add the live clams to the pan, then turn the heat up a little and add the white wine, place a lid on the pan. When the clams have opened, take the cooked spaghetti from the boiling water and add to the pan with the clams. Mix all together well, if it looks a little dry add a small cup-full of the water that you cooked the pasta in and mix well again heat the contents for about 3 minutes so that the pasta absorbs the flavour of the pan. Serve immediately.

Be very careful with the salt as the clams will release seawater which is salty.

Pasta con le Cozze

Pasta with Mussels

Here in Britain we are lucky to have access to some wonderful seafood and our mussels are among the best in the world. I like the contrast of the black shells of the mussels against the pale pasta.

Ingredients for 4

About 1 kilo of live mussels in shells

500 grams of linguine

Glass of white wine (dry)

One clove of garlic

Two tablespoons of chopped parsley

3 tablespoons of Olive oil

12 to 16 cherry tomatoes chopped in half

Salt and pepper to taste

Method

Take the mussels and place in a colander and wash under running water. Remove the 'beard' from the mussels and scrub the shells. Insure that the mussels all firmly closed.

Place a large pan of salted water onto boil.

In a large frying pan over a low heat add the olive oil and the garlic clove, when the garlic clove has gone soft remove and discard. By now the water will have come to a boil and you can add the pasta to cook to the boiling water. This will take ten or so minutes to cook.

Back to the frying pan and add the mussels and the white wine and cover with a lid, turn up the heat and shake the frying pan gently. Peep into the frying pan until you see the mussels opening. As soon as the mussels have opened remove the lid, turn the heat down and remove and discard at least two thirds of the mussel shells leaving behind the actual mussels.

You can now add the tomatoes to the frying pan. Cook on a medium heat until the tomatoes are slightly soft. Season the frying pan with salt and pepper to taste. By now the pasta should have cooked, if not then remove the frying pan from the heat for a few minutes until the pasta has cooked through. When al dente, drain the pasta into a colander and reserve some of the cooking water.

Add the drained pasta to the frying pan and add the chopped parsley while combining altogether. If the pasta looks a little dry then add some of the reserved water that the pasta was cooked in, stir again and then serve.

PASTA A LAMPADARIA

Lamp boat pasta

A summer evening, in the coastal village of Cersuta in Basilicata.

In the garden of Vincenzo's villa a humid and star filled night wrapped us in its warm embrace. The sound of crickets, the magic of fireflies, and the heavy scent of jasmine hanging in the air made for an unforgettable evening. From the vantage point of the villa above the sea, I sat watching the fishing boats in the Bay of Policastro. The boats came to a stop, and I could hear the sound of anchors sliding into the water. A few minutes later they switched on large lamps slung to the sides of the boats. The lights, which were turned downwards towards the water illuminated circles deep into the clear water. This was the method used since biblical times (without electric lights!) to catch anchovy. My friend Vincenzo said the boats are called Lampadaria meaning 'lamp boats' and when he was a boy in the 50's the local fisherman would go away to sea for up to two days from home, the boats were colourful but very basic and had no cooking facilities on board.

I asked Vincenzo what the men would eat while away and he replied 'Pasta a la Lampadaria' which the wives would lovingly cook for the men to take away with them and would then eat cold between slices of bread. Romance is cooking for those we love.

Ingredients for 4

Two handfuls of pitted black olives

One ball of mozzarella

One teaspoon of capers

½ a small medium red chilli

1 clove of garlic finely chopped

Large tablespoon of olive oil

Two tins of chopped tomatoes

Tomato paste how much?

3 chopped basil leaves

Salt and pepper

Method

In a heavy bottomed saucepan add two or three large tablespoon of the olive oil, chopped chillies and place on low heat. Add the chopped garlic taking care not to let the garlic burn, cook gently for 2 minutes.

Empty the contents of the tomato tins into the pan and add two large mugs of water to the saucepan. Cook on a low heat until the volume of the pan is reduced by half.

Add tomato paste to taste, along with the salt and pepper.

Heat a large pan of salted water to boil and add 500 grams of spaghetti to cook.

When pasta is cooked, drain and place in a large oven proof dish and add the tomato sauce, black olives, capers, basil leaves, chopped mozzarella, and mix well. Place dish into a preheated oven for 30 mins at 160c. Remove from the oven and serve. If you like you can leave it to go cold and take it on a picnic between slices of crusty bread.

Pasta e fagioli

Bean pasta

This really is wonderful pasta, cheap to make, tasty, and very satisfying. You can use runner or French beans; I think young tender runner beans are better. You'll need use fresh basil leaf for this recipe. This particular recipe needs fresh pasta and not dry, you can buy fresh pasta in most supermarkets or you can make your own.

Ingredients

Fresh pasta about 250grms for two persons

A good handful of tender runner beans or French beans chopped

One small-medium potato

Finely chopped leaf basil

Grated pecorino or parmesan cheese to taste

Method

Place a large pan of salted water on to boil for the pasta. Peel the potato and chop into small cubes. Then place chopped potatoes into a second pan and cover with salted water and cook until parboiled. Take the beans and chop to a similar size to the potatoes. Add the beans to the pan with the potatoes and cook until they are very tender and then drain and reserve.

Place the pasta into the boiling water and drain the pasta into a colander when cooked. Reserve some of the water used to cook the pasta. To a large frying pan add the beans and potatoes, then add the pasta, basil and the grated cheeses and mix well together. If the dish looks a little dry which it almost certainly will be, add some water from the pan in which the pasta was cooked. Stir well serve straight away.

Pasta Ragu

Ragu is the Sunday lunch of the south. It is a rich tomato sauce flavoured with cuts of meat and sausages which are cooked slowly over a low heat for up to three or four hours. It is the way I remember it made and the way I still make it now. The cuts of meat are typically just trimmings of pork, beef and sausages, sometimes chicken. When cooked the pasta is served with the sauce only, the meat being ladled out of the sauce and is served as a second course separately. In this booklet is a recipe for sausages which goes really well with this ragu.

Ingredients for 4

Two 400 gram tins of plum tomatoes

Two large garlic cloves, peeled

Four medium Italian sausages as in the menus

250 gm of silverside, diced

Two drumsticks

A few pork ribs cut into individual ribs

Glass of red wine

Basil, oregano, salt and black pepper to taste

Olive oil

Two tablespoons of tomato concentrate

500gm of pasta

Grated parmesan or pecorino cheese to taste

Method

In a large frying pan add a generous amount of olive oil, over a medium heat fry all the meat until browned. Take a large saucepan and pour in the contents of the frying pan and place saucepan on to a low heat. Add to this saucepan the tinned tomatoes, the garlic, and the herbs. Then fill the empty tomato tins with water and add to the sauce pan. Now add the tomato concentrate. Turn up the heat and bring to a slow boil then reduce the heat to simmer then add the wine. Continue to cook until the sauce reduces to just over one third. Stir often or it may burn. Keep adding water as necessary and aim to have just a third of the sauce left after about 3 hours. The meat should be falling apart. Bring a separate saucepan of salted water to the boil and the cook the pasta. While the pasta cooks remove the meat from the sauce and place aside in a warm oven. Drain the pasta and add to the saucepan of tomato sauce and add grated cheese, basil and oregano salt and pepper to taste. Stir well and if it is a little dry add some of the water from the pasta.

You can then serve the meat with some green bean salad.

Gnocchi

A choked priest, Samantha, and school boy romances

August 1974 and I seem to be spending a lot of time walking past one particular old house in Rogliano. Samantha lives in this house with her Mother and Grandmother. I notice that they sit out under the portico around 12 noon every day. I like Samantha; she gives me a big smile when I walk past, and she is simply gorgeous!

One week later, I just about summon up the courage to go over and say 'hello' when Samantha's mother calls out in Italian 'are you Franco from England'. The ice broken, I go over and introduce myself as politely as I can. It seems that Samantha's mother knows my Dad from their school days. Samantha and I end up most afternoons sitting together chatting beneath the shade of the portico under the watchful eye of Samantha's over protective grandmother. Some evenings we would go on a 'Passeggiata' together, an Italian evening ritual. It was the only time that we were almost alone, we could walk together about thirty yards ahead of her mother and grandmother, and at one particular bend in the road we would be 'out of line of sight' for a few seconds, and we would steal a quick kiss. We would giggle all the way back to her home while her grandmother would smile knowingly. (I think her grandmother knew that bend in the road as well.)

One afternoon Samantha's Grandmother said that they were cooking 'Sragolia Priti' (choked or strangled priests) and did I know what they were, 'yes' I said much to her surprise (I had helped my Mum cook these on numerous occasions). A short while later we sat around the kitchen table, on that table was a huge wicker basket which we used to press dimples and grooves into the Sragolia Priti before cooking them. They were all amazed at how well I could make them, I think I impressed them.

Samantha and I never met again. I returned to England and joined the Royal Navy, and Samantha left home to work in one of the Cities of Northern Italy. Sometimes the most innocent of memories are the sweetest.

Sragolia Priti (Gnocchi)

I believe that the name 'Sragolia Priti' came about after the greed of local priest, who was so enamoured with the dumplings which his housekeeper made that he cramped so many into his mouth that he choked to death. Gnocchi are simply dumplings made from boiled potatoes and flour, I think they are best served with a heavy tomato based sauce, the recipe of which you will find in this booklet. If you want a firmer dumpling then add an egg, but most prefer them without.

Ingredients

One large or two medium potatoes

Plain flour

Semolina for dusting

Salt

One medium free range egg

Method

Take the potatoes and wash them well, place the potatoes unpeeled into a large pan of salted water, bring the pan to the boil and then simmer till the potatoes are cooked through. Test with a small knife, it should go into the potatoes with no resistance. Remove from the water and let them cool.

When the potatoes have cooled you then need to peel them gently. When peeled mash or put them through a ricer into to a large bowl. It is at this point that you can add a beaten egg. Then take a handful of flour and mix together with the potatoes, keeping adding flour a handful at a time until you have formed a soft dough. At this point place the dough onto a flour dusted surface. With a knife cut off a large handful of the dough and roll it out into a long cylinder about a finger width wide. Cut the cylinder into small pieces about a thumbnail size then place on to a dusted surface. Continue this operation until all the dough is used up. You will now be left with little gnocchi that need finishing. Take one unfinished gnocchi and a fork, place the gnocchi it onto the top end of the fork tines and then with your index finger press down on to the gnocchi gently while drawing your finger down so as to roll the gnocchi down the tines of the fork. You should be left with the finished article, a little dumpling with a small indentation in it and grooved all the way round. Continue until all the gnocchi are finished. You will need to keep everything well dusted with flour.

To cook, place into a large pan of boiling water and remove when they rise to the surface. Place into a hot dish and cover with your favourite sauce. Ragu sauce as in this book is very good for this recipe.

Tortellini filled with spinach and ricotta

The priest, the housekeeper's sister, and tortellini

There was once a young priest who lived in a remote mountain village. His was the only church in the small village. The days were long and being the only priest he was kept busy. He was devoted to his flock and to his religion. As was tradition the priest was billeted into a home with a motherly, unattractive, but religious housekeeper. This ensured that no temptation would pass between them.

One day the housekeeper's young beautiful sister Maria came to visit from the north. The housekeeper introduced her sister to the priest who was working on his sermon in his study. As soon as the priest cast his eyes on her he fell completely under her spell. He started making excuses to meet and chat to her. He fought the conflicting emotions that raged in his mind. One day the priest overheard Maria say to her sister that she was going upstairs to have a bath. After a while the priest could no longer control himself and he crept tiptoeing up the stairs to the bathroom door. There he knelt down to look through the keyhole. Crestfallen, the only thing the priest could see was Maria's belly button, of which the priest thought the most wonderful object in the world. Now riven with guilt at what he done he went back to his study and prayed for forgiveness. A few days later Maria left to go back north and the priest was devastated. He walked into the kitchen, and on the table the housekeeper had left a sheet of homemade pasta cut into round circles. The priest looked at the pasta circle and had an idea. He took some ricotta cheese and placed it into the middle of the circle and then folded the circle over in half so as the filling was now inside a half moon. Then taking the half-moon with both his forefingers and thumbs he gently twisted the corners of the half-moon together until it formed the shape of Maria's belly button. And so the story goes that that is how 'Tortellini' came into to being.

<u>For four</u>

Ingredients

One beaten egg (optional)

Small tub of ricotta cheese

Small colander of washed spinach

Salt and pepper

Grated nutmeg

Two long sheets of homemade pasta (see homemade pasta)

Method

Wash the spinach well and place in a pan with two or three tablespoons of water, place on the heat and when well wilted remove the spinach and let cool. In a bowl add the ricotta and the cooled spinach. Add salt and pepper, and a little nutmeg to taste, and mix well together.

You can make the 'Tortellini' using squares of pasta as is the normal way, or round which I think are easier and better looking.

With a medium round biscuit cutter, cut out circles from the pasta sheet. Make about 6 to 7 tortellini for each person.

With a teaspoon, place a small amount of the mixture to just the bottom of centre of the pasta circle. Now with your finger or a pastry brush, place some of the beaten egg around the edge of the circle so that it will seal. You can use a little water to seal if you prefer. Fold the circle in half and seal well. Now comes the tricky bit, with forefingers and thumbs turn the two edges of the half-moon down towards each other. The upper edge of the half-moon should curl over, and the final shape should resemble a belly button! Place the tortellini into a pan of salted boiling water and as soon as they rise to the surface they are ready. Drain well and serve with a drizzle of very good virgin olive oil.

Pasta con Nduja

Nduja, was until recently, unknown outside of Calabria. It is a spreadable red hot pork sausage, more of a pate/paste in a natural casing. It has been mooted as one of the new great all time discoveries of Calabria. It is made from a wonderful pig call 'il nero di Calabria' a black medium sized pig. They roam free among the sweet chestnut trees that cover a lot of the hills and land of Calabria. They live a wonderful life for at least two years eating from the forest and its contents before they get the chop. The taste of Nduja is not easy to describe, it is sweet, but fiery hot, and never forgotten once tasted. Some of the best Nduja is made in La Sila, Calabria's national park.

Nduja does go wonderfully with tomato based pasta dishes. I like this recipe for its simple, honest and earthly ease of preparing and eating. I can promise you that you will go back again and again to eating this simple dish. Nduja is very hot. You may wish to start by adding one or maybe two teaspoons of Nduja first and see how it goes. Remember that you can easily add more, but it is much more difficult to take some away.

Ingredients for 4

Sixteen cherry tomatoes cut in half or five to six plum peeled tomatoes chopped

Two teaspoons of Nduja to start with

One large garlic clove finely chopped

Olive oil

Four teaspoons or more of grated pecorino cheese

500grms of Penne or similar pasta

Torn fresh basil leaves to taste

Salt and pepper to taste

Method

Place a large pan of salted water on to boil. In the mean time prepare the tomatoes, garlic and grate the cheese. When the water comes to the boil add the pasta. In a large frying pan add two or three glugs of olive oil. Place the frying pan onto a medium heat and add the tomatoes, garlic and nduja and fry gently and stir. When the tomatoes are soft and cooked through taste for salt and pepper and take pan off the heat until the pasta is just cooked to your liking.

Drain the pasta reserving some of the cooking water. Place the frying pan back on to a medium heat and add the pasta to the contents of the frying pan. Stir the pasta well into the Nduja and tomato sauce and if it looks a bit dry add some of the reserved cooking water. Add the pecorino cheese, torn basil leaves and give one last stir and then serve.

Nduja and Seafood pasta

Pasta ai frutti di mare con Nduja

A marriage made in heaven

Sometimes you come across something heavenly...

I present to you my idea of heaven on a plate. Tomatoes, sweet scallops, plump prawns, tender squid rings, and hot spicy pork Nduja. Ok, not really a cucina povera these days. But I like to think that some lucky fisherman would have made this dish now and again.

Ingredients for 4

4 scallops cut in half

250 grams of large shell on prawns peeled and prawn heads kept to one side

One medium sized squid prepared and cut into rings

Torn large basil leaves (6)

Six plum peeled tomatoes peeled and chopped

Two to four teaspoons of Nduja (depending on your taste for heat) Try two to start with.

Two glugs of olive oil

400-500 grams of linguine pasta

Salt and pepper to taste

Method

Place a large pan of salted water on to boil. While waiting for water to boil, prepare the ingredients. The easiest way to peel tomatoes is to pour boiling water from a kettle on them. In a large frying pan add the olive oil and place on a medium heat. Add all the prawn heads and fry gently stirring slowly for 5 minutes. With a potato masher crush the prawn heads so that all the juices are released. Pass the contents of the frying pan through a sieve pressing down the contents and collect the juices in a mug. Discard the prawn heads and pour he juices from the prawn heads back into the frying pan.

By now the water will have come to the boil; add the pasta to the boiling water to cook. Back to the frying pan and add the tomatoes and the nduja and place over a low heat stirring gently.

Once the tomatoes are soft add all the remaining ingredients except the basil to the frying pan and cook gently through. Remove frying pan from the heat while you wait a short while for the pasta to cook. Once the pasta is cooked, drain and reserve some of the cooking water. Place the frying pan back on the heat and pour in the drained pasta and stir well. If the pasta looks a bit dry add some of the reserved cooking water in which you cooked the pasta. Add the basil leaves stir briefly and serve.

Grilled sausages and peppers

A new admiral, a Fiat 128 and a trip into the mountains

It's an unusually cool November in Naples and Vesuvius is wearing a cap of snow. The cold crisp air hangs in the bay and the white capped volcano is reflected in the still blue waters of the bay. I really want to get out and go exploring. With the departure of dear Admiral MacDonald, a new Admiral has landed upon us with his family in tow, and consequently my cosy easy life has come to a rude end.

The new admiral's wife seems determined to host more dinner and cocktail parties then the entire fleet combined. Our working week goes from a relaxing twenty-five hours a week to a heart-breaking sixty-five hour week. Luckily most of our weekends are time off and I am determined to make the most of them. I've managed to get myself a car; it's an old white Fiat 128 with an 1100cc engine, it has orange and black striped seat covers, and black 'go faster' stripes along the sides and over its stubby bonnet. It's an odd car to buy as it is right hand drive and imported into Italy by an expat. I like to drive it fast, until the engine screams in protest. As most Neapolitan men think they are racing drivers, I tend to fit in quite well really. I had to take the new Admiral's wife into Naples and she had a 'vapour' at my driving! When she recovered she went and told the admiral who then tore a strip off me. I thought it was great fun, and I secretly think he thought so too. She never asked me for a lift again.

I've had the Fiat a fair few weeks now and I want to take the car out on a long drive. I have been told that in the Abruzzi national park there are Apennine wolves and wild bears. The bear are the last wild bears in Western Europe, I really want to visit. Like most young men I had a lot of misplaced trust in old cars, after all I have stuck go faster stripes all over it, so what could go wrong? I decide to ask my friends to come with me for the weekend, they are always up for some adventure, but they all decline. They think I'm as mad as the locals when I'm driving, let alone when up there in the mountains in the winter. I decide to see if I can charm some WRENS into coming, two or three will always fancy a ride out even if it's to just to get out of their quarters. But as soon as I tell them where I am going, they are all suddenly 'washing their hair' (How can it take a whole weekend to wash your hair?) I'm starting to get that 'Billy no-mates' feeling. I decide to head out on my own.

Very early one Saturday morning sees me setting off out of Naples and the two and a half hour journey to the Abruzzi national park. I take a light jacket just in case, after all it's 14 degrees C here in the bay of Naples. Driving through Naples on an early weekend morning is like watching a dormant giant waiting to wake up and cause mayhem. I head out of the city and north onto the Autostrada. Then will strike out toward Caserta, and then on to Casino where I will leave the motorway behind and head inland and due north east. At the toll booth near Casino a disinterested attendant waves me through as he is too lazy to stretch across my right hand drive car to collect the toll, handy that. Approaching the town of Casino I catch a glimpse of the abbey up on the hill, it looks spectacular and as the early morning sun strikes the abbey it glows red, it can be seen from miles away. I decide to take a look and follow the unnecessary signs to this majestic sight.

As I climb up the hill and approach the abbey, I see the vast Polish War Cemetery and my happy little world comes to a sudden halt. Words are just not enough to describe the sacrifice made on this most holy of sites by allies thousands of miles away from home to free Italy from tyranny; I don't need to say more.

At the abbey I leave my car in a deserted car park and take a walk around, it's early and I think I am the only visitor. I wonder into the abbey and I hear the most wonderful sound, the abbots are singing, and it is indescribably moving. I have never heard such a beautiful sound, and probably never will again. I open a large engraved brass door and the scene and sound just takes me away. I stand in the doorway for a half a minute or so and then retreat back outside, I feel as if I am intruding in a special moment for the monks.

Back on to my journey I make my way ever higher, near the small town of Atina surrounded by oak and beech covered hills, I stop at a small farm selling cheese and buy some ricotta from an old lady. It comes in a wicker basket, she tells me it has just been made, and I find it's still warm. The old lady offers me some homemade bread and I accept it. I drive a bit further up the road, stop, and I breakfast on some of the warm creamy ricotta and bread, what a breakfast!

Strange, but I'm sure it's getting colder and if I'm not wrong I think that there is snow on those hills further up. As I climb up further away from Atina the snow line comes ever closer and then all of a sudden I am surrounded by deep snow on both sides of the road. The trees are draped in snow. The road is reasonably clear but very icy in places. In the distance I can see mountain peaks covered in snow. Then a sign appears, 'welcome to the Abruzzi national park'. A while after I pass the sign the car seems to be struggling up the hill, a mile or so later it starts to misfire and then comes to a stop.

Oh no! I try to restart the engine but the cars having none of it. I get out of the car, its freezing cold, and it can't be more than two degrees C. I open the bonnet and gawp down vacantly at the engine. I look about me and there's not a living soul around, not a sound, I am surrounded by forest, then I remember about the wolves! My senses are on full alert, and then I think I can smell wood smoke so decide to investigate. I walk warily up the road, looking out for a pack of crazed wolves ready to jump out of the woods to eat me. I'm busting for a pee, but there's no way on this earth I'm going to do that, the thought of those wolves, and me in that predicament, no, no way! I haven't gone three hundred yards and at a bend in the road I see a ramshackle collection of low buildings: salvation. I walk towards the buildings and find that there is a restaurant come café, come bar, come whatever you like. It's crazy; it's all over the place, benches and chairs under a lean to roof of corrugated iron. A fire pit burns warmly, and next to it is a long BBQ with chickens grilling, and long thin sausages. The man who I think is the owner comes out and asks what I want, I tell him I have broken down and was worried about the wolves, he starts to laugh and calls out to whom I think is his wife and they both start laughing, and they tell me I have more chance of landing on the moon then being eaten by wolves. He telephones a friend who will come out to fix the car, and while I wait he asks what I would like to eat. The sausages look good so I have them, fresh off the oak embers. I sit down to the sausages, with some grilled red peppers. The flavours of the oak grilled sausages are as good as it gets a mix of fennel, pork and black pepper. Sitting there eating the hot sausages and grilled peppers surrounded by snow is a memory that I will treasure. I am happy to report that this restaurant is still open you can visit online at: www.ristoroforcadacero.it/

These sausages are a general description of sausages made all over the south of Italy, they vary from region to region but they share the same characteristics. They should on no account be confused with the sausages sold in our supermarkets. The ingredients are all good quality. Please use pork from a reputable butcher, and natural sausage casings. If this is your first time at sausage making use a funnel and your thumb to fill the casing. You can buy an attachment for a mixing machine, or if you're really keen you can buy a sausage stuffer. The amount of pork used looks a lot, but if you're going to the trouble of making sausages, then you might as well go the whole hog! Remember that you can freeze them.

Ingredients

1 kilo of course, minced shoulder of pork

1 kilo of minced fatty belly of pork

Two mugs of bread crumbs (optional)

2 teaspoons of toasted fennel seeds (toast gently in a dry frying pan)

Dried chilli flakes to taste (optional)

2 teaspoons of cracked black pepper

Grated nutmeg to taste

A glass of red wine with alcohol boiled off (optional)

Salt to taste

Natural sausage casings

Method

In a bowl of warm water place the sausage casings to soak. In a separate large bowl mix all the ingredients together well by hand. Take a small amount of the mix and make a mini burger and fry gently until cooked, taste the mini burger and adjust any seasonings before proceeding.

You need breadcrumbs because the pork sold in the UK is quite lean compared to the pork sold in southern Italy, lean pork can make the sausages a bit dry. The bread crumbs help to keep the sausage moist.

Take the soaked casings and run water from the tap through them and then tie a small knot in one end. Then roll the casing onto the end of your stuffer and start to fill the casing with the sausage mix until all the mix is used up. You should now have a very long sausage.

Take the long sausage and tie a knot in the casing opposite end to the start of the sausage. Now decide how long you like your sausages to be, twist the end of sausage round to the right and then twist the next end sausage to the left, twist left and right until you have all your sausages.

Your sausages are now made and I would leave them in the fridge for at least a day to let the flavours develop. Freeze what you are not going to eat. I think these sausages are best baked in the oven or even better on a bbq of oak embers. Share with friends, in the knowledge that you know what's gone into them. Serve with the peppers below.

Roasted or grilled red peppers

This recipe is very popular all over southern Italy; often following a summer glut of peppers many people will preserve the roasted peppers in large and small jars.

Red peppers (1 kilo)

Olive oil

Pine nuts, two tablespoons

Red wine vinegar or balsamic to taste

Salt and pepper to taste

Method

First of all you have to remove the tough shiny skin from the peppers, this is no easy task and the methods range from using a blowtorch to roasting in a very hot oven till the skin is charred. I find that placing them under a grill or better still on a very hot griddle until the skin chars the best way. By the time the skin has charred the peppers will be cooked. Leave to cool in a bowl and then peel the skin off gently. Place the peeled peppers and any juices into a bowl and add the pine nuts. Drizzle over some olive oil and vinegar to your taste and season with salt and pepper. Leave for the flavours to develop for a few hours then enjoy on their own with Bread or with some grilled meat.

If you want to preserve the peppers then follow the recipe above and place into sterilized jars and lids that have been cleaned and boiled in water. When you have filled the jar, top up with sunflower oil and screw the lid on tight. Place the filled and sealed jars back into boiling water for five minutes and then remove. The lid will be firm and will not 'pop' if the lid is pressed; this indicates that it is airtight. They should keep for months, but always check the seal before opening and eating. Once open consume within a few days.

Scallopini de Manzo

Beef Escallops

This recipe is an ideal way of making meat go a very long way, it will impress your friends, it tastes fantastic, and it costs so little to make. Make your own breadcrumbs from stale bread, slice the bread up and leave out in the room to dry out. When the bread has dried completely put it into a food processor and blitz, alternatively place the slices into a plastic bag and beat with a rolling pin. You can use this recipe and exchange the beef, for chicken, pork, or veal. For a vegetarian, exchange the meat for sliced Aubergines.

Ingredients for 4

½ a kilo of rump steak

Two beaten eggs

One mug of fine breadcrumbs

½ a mug of plain flour

Salt and pepper to season

Chopped parsley

Finely chopped garlic clove

Oregano

Method

Cut any fat away from the meat. Then cut the meat into four pieces. Take each piece of meat in turn and place between two sheets of cling film. With a meat hammer slowly but firmly bash the meat out thinly so that it is no more than five mm thick. If the bashed out beef is a bit large then please cut them in two. Place the bashed out slices into the fridge. Then take three bowls and place the flour, breadcrumbs, and the beaten eggs in to each bowl separately.

Season the flour well with salt and pepper. Add some chopped parsley, oregano and the chopped garlic to the breadcrumbs just enough to speckle the breadcrumbs.

In a shallow frying pan add plenty of sunflower oil and place onto a medium heat. Take a slice of the meat or two and dust it in the flour, then dip into the beaten egg and then pat it on to the breadcrumbs so that the meat is well coated. Place the coated meat into the frying pan and cook until golden, turning the meat over both sides. Keep the meat warm while you cook the remaining slices. Serve immediately with wedges of lemon and a crisp salad.

Frittata de patata e verdure

Potato and vegetable omelette

Everyone it seems is talking about 'frittata' as if it is something edgy and 'out-there' it's just an omelette in Italian style. I like this recipe because it uses only vegetables and with a few fresh herbs it describes 'cucina povera' perfectly on a plate.

Ingredients for four hungry people

Three or four medium potatoes, peeled and thinly sliced

One or two large red onion(s), peeled and sliced

One or two courgette(s), sliced

Torn basil leaves to taste

Large handful of parsley, roughly chopped

Pinch of fennel seeds (optional)

Three or four medium eggs, whisked

Salt and pepper to taste

Olive oil

Method

Pour out two or three tablespoons of olive oil into a large heavy bottomed frying pan and place onto a low heat. Add the sliced potatoes and the onions and fry gently for a few minutes, then cover the pan with a lid. When the potatoes are soft add the courgettes, basil leaves, parsley and fennel seeds and continue to cook until the courgettes are cooked. Arrange the contents of the pan into a uniform level round shape and pour the whisked eggs into the pan. You have now created a 'frittata' not an English omelette. You may not be able to flip the frittata in the frying pan as it will be too heavy. With a spatula turnover parts of the frittata until it is cooked, don't worry if it breaks up because it probably will. It is all part of the character of this frittata. Serve promptly on warm plates.

Neapolitan Pizza

A Scottish Admiral, a stray dog, WRENS, and Neapolitan Pizza

In 1978 I had the very good fortune to get a secondment to work In Naples for NATO, and the British Admiral living in Posillipo. I got this on the back of the fact I could speak Italian, and that I had relatives living nearby. So there I was, 19 years old, and living in Pozzuoli just outside Naples. I was furnished with my own flat, and all bills paid for by the MOD. My problems began when I had to get myself from where I lived in Pozzuoli, to the Admirals house in the very upmarket area of Posillipo. For the first month or so till I got a car, I had to get two buses to Posillipo. The second bus was driven by what I can only describe as a lunatic with a licence; He would take the hairpin bends with complete suicidal contempt for his passengers. Over the next few weeks I got to know him, and he could not get his head around the fact that this Italian looking and speaking passenger would board the bus in a Royal Navy uniform. This confusion was to follow me for the two years I spent in Naples. Italian Navy personnel would scratch their heads in confusion.

Admiral MacDonald was a larger than life figure. He was a complete Gentleman in every sense of the word, and he inspired everyone around him. He was a wonderful man to work for, people would do anything for him, and he was a fantastic artist. He was unmarried, and so for his house staff of four, including me, it was a job made in heaven. I was promoted shortly after arriving in Naples to a Leading rate, but as I worked in his house and the other three staff were all petty officers or above I ended up getting all the jobs the others did not want.

It was a wonderful life, sunshine, fantastic food, and loads of time off. When I was on duty I would turn up at 6am to get the Admirals Uniform and his breakfast ready. One morning, I opened the front door and was greeted by a barking, flea infested puppy. The Admiral was sat on a stool looking completely knackered and bleary eyed. He had been up all night looking after this dog. The night before, while out for a walk he had found him abandoned in the local park and had taken him home. The Admiral had named him 'Salvo' short for Salvato or the saved one, and little did I know at the time just how much trouble Salvo would give me. The Chief Petty officer, despised Salvo, the CPO and PO Stewards barely tolerated Salvo, and every time Salvo did something wrong (which was most days) I got it in the neck. Salvo would end up being looked after by me every time the Admiral had to go away. The Admiral would not ask me, he would just say 'you will have Salvo won't you'

That meant no going out at night as Salvo would always create mayhem, and if left alone would tear up the furniture. Taking him out with me was not an option as he would always try and bite a local! So Salvo got his way, while my friends would be out with the girls.

Naples was a city fully alive, it was slightly frightening, dirty, noisy, but the people were amazingly friendly and hospitable. I made a friend of my own age who was an airman in the RAF, and we would spend weekends driving miles and miles in each other's cars sightseeing. Sometimes if we were lucky we would somehow manage to talk a couple of WRENS mad enough into coming with us, and some weekends would see us collecting them from their quarters on the NATO base. On Friday nights we would all go to a Pizzeria in Arco, which had a huge wood burning oven and cooked the most fantastic Pizza's with buffalo mozzarella cheese. Laughter, and red wine would flow, and god only knows how we managed to drive the girl's home. Pizza Margarita was my favourite; it was simply tomatoes, mozzarella, and basil. It would come out of the wood burner sizzling hot, and the dough was soft and bubbly, it was a taste explosion in the mouth. I wanted to know how to make them. Over time, I got to know the proprietor and he gave me the recipe that I will describe.

Admiral Macdonald moved back to the Isle of Skye, and at great expense took Salvo with him. Salvo the Neapolitan stray ended up on a Scottish Island!

Pizza Napolitana

Ingredients

½ Kilo of '00' flour Plain white

250grm of semolina

Natural yeast or instant dried yeast

2-3 pinches of salt

Water

6 Fresh bell tomatoes peeled, chopped, and puréed

Buffalo Mozzarella cheese

Fresh Basil leaves

Large terracotta tile or oven stone

Method

The secret to a good Pizza is to keep it simple, and don't put too much on it, pizza is best with less on top. I will describe the making of Pizza Margarita, as a variation to this you can substitute the Basil for Oregano, and add salted Anchovies and cappers for a Pizza Marinara.

To make the dough, add both of the flours to a mixing bowl or to an electric mixer. Add the required amount of natural yeast to a small amount of water and wait until it has activated before adding it to the flour. Or add the instant dried yeast to the weight of flour as instructed on the packet into the flour. Turn the machine on low, and add the salt. Then slowly add water to the mix until it has formed a smooth dough that leaves the sides clean. Keep mixing for at least eight minute on a medium speed; ensure that this mixing does not introduce to much heat to the dough. The dough should be elastic. Cover the dough in an oiled bowl with cling film and place somewhere warm for about 2-3 hours.

Prepare the tomatoes by peeling, chopping and pureeing. Then add salt and pepper to taste.

When the dough is nearly ready, place the oven stone or terracotta tile into the oven and preheat the oven to the highest setting you can. (If you have a wood burning oven then light it 50mins before you need it) Take the dough gently knead by hand on a floured surface. Cut a piece of dough about a size smaller than a tennis ball and with your hands flatten the dough out to a round disk about 8 to 10 inches across on a very well dusted surface (use the semolina flour) Don't worry if it's slightly out of shape. Place the disk down onto a dusted surface and add 3-4 tablespoons of the tomato puree on to the dough and with the back of the spoon spread the tomato puree in a circle over the pizza base. Then add the mozzarella cheese lightly over the surface to your own taste, but don't add too much. Tear the basil leaves on to the base. Then add some salt and pepper to taste on to the pizza, and lastly

Carefully place the pizza directly on to the oven stone in the oven, or place it into the wood burner. The pizza will not take long to cook. In a wood burner it will cook in about 60-90 seconds, in an oven it can take up to 10-12 minutes. Remove from the oven and serve. You can make at least 6 pizzas with a kilo of flour. If you are making just one or two Pizzas you can place the left over dough into the freezer for use later.

STUFFED EGG PLANT

Ingredients for 4

3 tablespoons of olive oil

1/2 of a small, medium hot chilli pepper chopped finely

One cup of heavy tomato sauce (from this booklet)

2 large aubergine

250 grams of minced pork

2 clove of garlic, finely chopped

2 large hand full of large leaf parsley, finely chopped

100 grams of grated parmigano cheese

Salt and pepper

Cut the two eggplants in half from top to bottom cutting through the stalk if you wish. With a spoon carefully scoop out most of the inside white flesh of all four eggplant halves leaving the purple casings which you will later fill. Then turn the oven on to 180c.

Roughly chop up the flesh of the eggplants into small cubes, place in a colander and sprinkle generously with salt. This process should remove any bitterness from the eggplant. After about 20 min remove the chopped eggplant and gently squeeze out any liquid. In a medium frying pan add the olive oil and preheat before adding the chopped eggplants and fry gently for about 10 min. Remove from the frying pan place into a large bowl, and then add the pork, garlic, parsley, parmigiano cheese, and the chilli, then mix well together. Return this mixture to the eggplant casings sharing out so they are equality filled.

Place the filled eggplants into a baking dish and the pour some tomato sauce onto the top to the mixture in each eggplant half.

Place into the oven for about 30 mins or until well browned and cooked through, or if you are lucky, into a wood burning oven.

Aurata

Grilled Sea Bream, and the fable of the old fisherman

Many years ago, an old man lived in a converted cave on a beach in Calabria. He would fish with a simple rod for his supper, and he would grill the fish he caught on the beach, and any extra fish he could not eat, he would barter for goods with the locals. One day a rich businessman was walking along the beach. Seeing the old man fishing, the rich man strikes up a conversation with him. Surprised at how the old man lives, he asked him why he did not buy two rods so that he could catch twice as many fish. The old man looks at the rich man and asks 'then what'? The rich man responds that then, he could sell the extra fish, and have more money. The old man looks confused and the businessman adds that then then he can buy a boat and catch even more fish; buy a bigger boat with an engine and you could catch even more fish. The old man still doesn't understand, and with exasperation the businessman explains that then he could employ people, he would no longer have to work, and could have a life of ease. The old man scratches his head and simply replies, 'why would I want to go all through that, to achieve what I am already doing'.

Grilled Sea Bream

(Sold as Greek sea bream)

Ingredients

Two bream filleted skin left on.

Half a lemon

Fresh mint

Olive oil

Salt and pepper to taste

Method

This is as simple a recipe that one could hope for, if you are happy you can fillet them yourself, or ask your fishmonger to fillet them for you.

On a baking tray pour out 3 to 4 tablespoons of olive oil on to the tray, then place the fillets skin side down on to the baking tray, drizzle some more olive oil over the top of the fillets, squeeze the lemon over all the fillets, then place under a very hot grill until the fish is just cooked through. Tear some fresh mint over the fish while it's still in the tray and wait a few minutes for the mint to wilt. Then serve. You can serve this with a bean salad.

Pollo in Padella

Fried chicken with lemon and orange zest

A simple dish full of the flavours and fragrance of the Mediterranean makes this dish ideal on a summer or winter evening.

Ingredients

One whole chicken chopped up into segments

Zest of one lemon

Zest of one orange

1 sprig of rosemary

Olive oil

Plain flour

Two garlic cloves

Salt and pepper

½ a glass of dry white wine

Method

In a large heavy bottomed frying pan add a generous amount of olive oil. Place pan on a medium heat. In a large bowl add sufficient well-seasoned flour to dust the chicken segments. Dust and then place the chicken to the frying pan and brown the chicken well.

When the chicken has turned golden turn down the heat. Add the white wine, the zests, the garlic and the rosemary and cook over a gentle heat. If the pan looks dry add some chicken stock to the pan. When the chicken is cooked, serve with a light vegetable salad as described in this booklet.

Calabrian meatballs

HMS Antrim, the officers mess, and Calabrian meatballs

I am almost eighteen years old, it's the mid-seventies, and I have been on my first ship for six month. HMS Antrim is a guided missile destroyer, and on deployment in the Mediterranean. I am so proud and idealistic as only the young can be. Antrim is a happy ship, and a lucky ship, in an age of defence cuts we are lucky to be on the first of two major deployments that will see us in the Seychelles, the Suez Canal, and then across the Atlantic to the Caribbean as the guard ship to the Royal Yacht! I am looking forward to docking in Naples. All my mates want to go ashore with me as I can speak the lingo. I am staring out of the porthole in the officer's wardroom, daydreaming of going ashore and all the places we are visiting, the sun is blazing, and the sea is an incredible blue. I think to myself that I could take the lads to a real Neapolitan Pizzeria. All of a sudden Taff the leading Steward Says 'Oi Frank, get your ass moving round the tables and collect the empty plates, for f**** sake stop day dreaming' I turn a bright red, I was easily embarrassed at that age. I run round the tables picking up the empty plates, and a spotty faced midshipman says to me with a barely concealed smirk 'looking forward to Taranto night, Altomare?' No I'm not looking forward to Taranto night; it's all hard work for us stewards. The young midshipman thinks I will be pissed off by them celebrating the sinking of the Italian Navy, I feel like telling him where to stick it, but for one, I am not going to lower myself to his level, and second, I don't want to spend the night locked up and on a charge. I give him an ironic smile instead. Lucky for me, a senior officer overhears him, and takes him out of the wardroom. Ten minutes later they walk back in, and now it's the midshipman who is bright red, seeing him red faced gave me a nice warm glow inside.

We don't make it to Naples, and we sail on to Alexandria in Egypt instead! Everyone is disappointed especially me, I was really looking forward to showing off my Italian to the lads in my mess deck. A few days later, the officer that stuck up for me says that it would be nice to have an Italian meal as we did not make it to Naples, and asks me what I would have, I said a nice plate of pasta and meatballs would be really nice. He asked me if I would be willing to help the cooks prepare it. I jump at the chance. Two nights later, a very proud seventeen year old is looking at all the empty plates coming back into the pantry. I was really pleased, and guess what? It was Taranto night the next night, and I was given the night off. Oh and the midshipman refused the pasta, what an idiot.

Polpette a sugo di pomadoro

Calabrian meatballs in heavy tomato sauce

Ingredients

Half a kilo of lean beef mince

Two mugs of bread crumbs

½ of one small medium hot red chilli chopped finely

A large hand full of flat leaf parsley

One cup of gradated parmesan or pecorino cheese

Two eggs

Salt and pepper to taste

Method

In a large mixing bowl add all the ingredients together and combine well with your hands. There should emanate a wonderful smell of parsley and cheese. From this mixture, take a small amount and shape into a round ball a little larger than a marble, continue until the mixture is all used up. You can if you wish make larger meatballs, but I like the smaller ones, they look more elegant on the plate.

In a large frying pan add some cooking oil about 1cm deep, place on the heat, when the oil is hot place the meatballs into the hot oil to brown, when browned remove from the heat and drain on kitchen paper. You should then add these meatballs to the heavy tomato sauce as described earlier, and cooked in the sauce for as long as you cook the sauce, this will impart a wonderful flavour to the sauce.

Polpette di riso

A variation on aranchini

Rice balls

I really like this recipe; it is simple rustic food, it is in the best traditions of Calabrians making food go a long way. It is cheap to make, but so tasty and wholesome.

Ingredients

1 mug of arborio rice

Cup of grated parmesan cheese or pecorino

One large egg beaten

2 handfuls of flat leaf parsley

Salt and pepper to taste

2 mugs of water or chicken stock (optional)

Method

You need to cook the rice as if you were making a risotto preferably the day before, you can cook the rice using chicken stock or you can use plain water. In a large pan add 2 tablespoons of olive oil, heat the pan gently, then add the rice stirring until the rice is well coated. Add the water or chicken stock all at once and bring to the boil, once water is boiling, lower heat to a simmer. When the rice is tender it should have absorbed all or most of the liquid. Remove from the heat and drain off any excess water. Leave the rice to cool in the fridge for a day.

The next day when you are ready remove the rice from the fridge and add the beaten egg, the Parmesan, and the parsley.

Mix together by hand till well combined, if too dry add more beaten egg. Add salt and pepper to taste. You should be able to form a simple round ball shape about the size of a golf ball.

Carefully deep fry the formed rice balls into the hot oil and fry until golden. Remove from the pan and drain well on some kitchen paper, then serve immediately. You can as a variation add a small cube of mozzarella cheese to the centre of the ball.

Calabrian pan fried rabbit

Italian men, the lady animal lover, and Calabrian pan fried rabbit

In the early 1960s my Dad and I step down off a high footpath in Maidenhead that elevates the path above any floods from the Thames. We cross the road together over to a lovely bungalow surrounded by roses and wisteria. As we reach the other side of the road I jump up and down in excitement, my Dad's going to get me a rabbit! I've never had a pet before.

Outside of the bungalow on the garden fence is a large sign saying 'RABBITS FOR SALE'. I run up and open the wrought iron front gate, tear up the gravel footpath and then on towards the front door and knock. The large oak door is opened by a slim lady in her 70s with grey curly hair who peers down at me over her spectacles with a lovely smile; she is dressed in a floral print dress with pink slippers. 'We've come to buy a rabbit' I squeal, 'Oh how jolly nice' she replies.

We follow her to the back garden were a large old shed has been converted in to a comfortable home for what are obviously well loved animals. My dad is asked to choose from about a dozen rabbits of different colours. I want the little white one, but my Dad chooses the largest one that is a boring dull brown. My Dad hands over a few pennies and as we walk away he is delighted at the price, the rabbit on the other hand stares forlornly out of its box, and it does not look very delighted at all.

I love looking after the rabbit and ask my Dad when he will build a hutch. A few days later and the box is empty, and I wonder at what happened to the bunny. My dad says it's gone to heaven? I'm not too sure myself? 'Never mind' my dad says, we can get a new one tomorrow. My Dad is in the garden of our house, when one of his Italian friends comes around and says thank you to him for putting him on to the bargain rabbits. Over the course of the next few months or so my dad and his friends buy more rabbits, but strangely they all end up in bunny heaven after a few days. My friend Giovanni confirms that the same sad fate happens to his rabbits? One day my dad and I are at the old lady's bungalow and my dad is buying a new rabbit. By now all the rabbits have learnt to huddle into a corner and try to disappear behind each other. The old lady exclaims that Italians seem to love rabbits, and that my dad must have about six of them by now. My dad looks at her quickly and says 'No, I no have any'. Visibly shocked the lady asks what's happened to them, to which my dad replies 'I eat them all, datsa what happen' And it is at this moment that the old lady goes mad, quite totally raving mad, and starts screaming and frothing at the mouth, grabbing the rabbit back, and goes to fetch a broom. My dad gets the message and we run out of her gate with my dad swearing in Italian that she's bloody crazy. A few days later as we walk past the bungalow there is a large sign has been edited and now reads 'RABBITS FOR SALE, NO ITALIANS'

I am not sure that there is a particular recipe called 'Calabrian Rabbit', but this is the recipe cooked by my family, I am sure that it is one of those recipes that change from family to family.

Rabbit is very lean with little or no fat so that it is a very healthy food. Rabbit can be dry, so needs to be cooked in a liquid, white wine is good.

Calabrian pan fried rabbit

Ingredients

One skinned and quartered rabbit for two persons

Two garlic cloves peeled

Well-seasoned flour for dusting

Cheap olive oil to fry

Sprig of rosemary

150-200 grams of lardons of bacon or chopped pancetta

Two glasses of white dry white wine

¼ of red chilli pepper chopped (optional)

Salt and pepper to taste

Handful of chopped flat leaf parsley

Method

Ask your butcher to skin and quarter the rabbit for you, this will save you becoming sentimental or squeamish about bunny.

In a small sauce pan add the white wine and heat till it boils, turn down to a simmer for two minutes then take off the heat. This will remove any acidic taste from the wine. Take a large heavy bottomed frying pan and add about 3 or four good glugs of olive oil Turn on to a low heat and add the garlic, chilli and the rosemary, heating gently in the pan. When the garlic has softened remove it from the pan. Take the rabbit and place in a bowl and dust all over in the flour and then place the rabbit into the frying pan and turn up the heat, fry the rabbit until it has gone a light golden colour. Now add the lardons or pancetta and turn the heat down to low. Add the white wine and the chilli and continue to cook for about 20 minutes or so with a lid over the frying pan. You may need to add a little water during the cooking if the pan looks dry. Now add salt and pepper to taste. You should a lovely sauce at the bottom of the pan to serve with the rabbit. This dish goes well with new potatoes, or some steamed broccoli.

Verdure ai ferri

Grilled vegetables

Ingredients for four as a starter or two as a main

One large eggplant

Two courgettes

Twelve mushrooms

Sunflower oil

Olive oil

Balsamic vinegar

Garlic clove

Dry chilli flakes

Salt and pepper to taste

Small handful of mint leaves

Method

For this recipe you need to have a cast iron griddle plate which will fit over the cookers gas burners. If you do not have a griddle plate then you could use a BBQ. The griddle will need to be very hot, so put the griddle on and turn the gas burners under the griddle to high. Whilst waiting for the griddle to get hot you can start to prepare the vegetables. Cut the eggplant and courgettes into round slices about 5 mm thick, and then place them in a bowl a splash some sunflower oil over them and toss them with the oil. Place the eggplant slices first onto the griddle and turn the heat down to medium low. While waiting for them to sear, chop the mushrooms in half and again toss them in some sunflower oil. When the eggplants have char-lines they will need to be turned over and char-lined on the other side. When both sides of the eggplants are char-lined remove them to a serving bowl and repeat the process with the courgettes and the mushrooms. Dress with olive oil and balsamic vinegar and sprinkle with some dried chilli flakes to taste. Serve cold.

Vegetable Salads

Salads are an integral part of Italian food; here are a few salads which go well with some of the main courses in this booklet.

Green bean salad

Use any type of tender green beans, chopped garlic, olive oil, salt and pepper to taste, and good quality balsamic vinegar.

First cook the beans till tender in salted boiling water. Remove from the boiling water and plunge into cold water. Drain and let cool. When cool sprinkle with the chopped garlic and dress with olive oil and the vinegar. Mix well together and serve.

Cauliflower salad, with mint.

Cut the cauliflower into florets and place into to boiling salted water and cook till tender. Then drain and plunge into cold water. Drain and allow to cool. Place in a serving dish and sprinkle with chopped mint leaves, and dress with olive oil and white wine vinegar.

Tomato salad

Use beefsteak tomatoes if you can. Cut the tomatoes in half and arrange on a serving dish. Season with salt, sprinkle with oregano, and drizzle over with olive oil and a little red wine vinegar. Leave for at least 20mins to marinate before serving.

Marinated mushrooms.

You can use button mushrooms for this wonderful salad. The mushrooms are marinated and not cooked.

Take 500grms of small button mushrooms, place in a bowl and add one chopped garlic clove, half a chopped red onion, chopped flat leaf parsley, and salt and pepper to taste. To this mix add half a generous measure of olive oil and white wine vinegar and mix well together and place in the fridge for at least two hours before serving. The mushrooms will be marinated and do not need cooking.

Tuna in oil

This recipe is a preserving method that leaves the tuna tender and flaky, it is not to be confused with tinned tuna, and the tuna is preserved in sterilized jars in olive/sunflower oil. The tuna from this recipe goes really well with a salad of fresh sliced cherry tomatoes and cracked green olives.

Ingredients

1 kilo of fresh tuna steak

Olive oil

Sunflower oil

Method

Place the tuna steak in a large pan containing 5 litres of cold water. Add about 250grm of salt to the pan and place on to the heat and bring slowly to the boil. When the water is boiling turn the heat down to simmer for about 1 hour. Remove the tuna from the water and leave on a plate somewhere cool to dry. Whilst drying place some jam jars or preserving jars and the lids into a pan of boiling water and leave them for at least 10 minutes. Remove jars from the water and drain. When the tuna has cooled cut in to bite sized chunks and place into the sterilized jars. When the jars are full top them up with a 50/50 mix of olive oil and sunflower oil. Replace the lids firmly on to the filled jars and place the filled jars back in to the pan that you used to sterilize the jars. Bring the water to boil again for at least 15 minutes and then remove. The tuna in the jars are now preserved and can be kept until needed, once the jar is opened then they must **be placed in the fridge.**

Salami

10 pin bowling, a mafia shooting, and homemade Salami

Amantea on the west coast of Calabria was many years ago one of the most enchanting towns on coast. The old town sat under a castle high up on a hill by the sea, where colourful open fishing boats were pulled up onto a pebbly beach and local fisherman passed the time of day mending nets and chatting. Today Amantea is a modern vibrant town with lots of interesting restaurants and shops to explore and is justifiably popular. The old byzantine castle still casts a wary eye on proceedings in the new town, and it's a worthwhile walk to the old town and is always good for a wonderful view.

It is a warm summer evening in Amantea, and in the bowling alley is Roberto and his wife, some friends, and with them visiting, are my sister and her very English husband Malcolm. They are happily playing bowls and having a great time looking forward to a pizza before they go home. Roberto is not known for his patience and when they run out of bowls he asks the man in the alley next to him if he can use some of his as they are only two of them, and nine of his party. The man who is as pig-headed as Roberto says no. Roberto who is more than old enough to know better, gets into an argument. The two men then start to trade insults, when the man walks away Roberto follows him to the shoe counter, a bit of pushing and pulling takes place, when all of a sudden, Roberto head-butts the man on the nose, blood pours from him, and he runs out dragging his screaming wife with him. Roberto walks back to his friends who call him a bloody fool and say they should leave. Roberto is having none of it and is determined to finish the game.

15 minutes later they are just finishing the game when the man with the bloody nose walks into the bowling alley and marches strait up to Roberto, in his hand is a revolver, he aims the revolver at Roberto's legs and shoots from 5ft away, the first 2 shots unbelievably miss! Three others hit him in his leg, one of the shots that miss hits Malcolm in his ankle. Pandemonium breaks out, women are screaming, children are crying, and men are running around bumping into each other like headless chickens. Thankfully someone has the good sense to call for an ambulance. Luckily for Roberto and Malcolm, by some miracle the bullets do not pass through any bones or arteries. Both are in shock, and in the melee the Gunman disappears. The two are taken away to hospital. The police cordon off the area and start to interview everyone in the bowling alley. Amazingly no one has seen a thing; no one knows anything, nobody knows the gunman or has ever seen him before. It slowly dawns on my sister, their friends, and the police who the gunman might be. After days of interviews and photo fits, countless interviews of locals, the police draw blanks. The two victims are lucky, after a week Malcolm is released from hospital and a month later so is Roberto. Roberto goes home, and keeps a very low profile for a while until the police inform him that if the gunman had wanted him dead, he would have been dead the night of the shooting.

The police never discovered who the gunman was, but six months later a huge police operation in the Amantea area nets about forty members suspected of belonging to an organized crime syndicate. The bowling alley is raided, and shut down, so is the Marina, and other fringe businesses also disappear.

I visited Roberto about a year later at his villa; in his cellar hang the most wonderful salami you can imagine. All home-made, I wanted to make some salami myself for years, and we discussed the best way to make them. He gave me a lot of guidance that has proved invaluable. Homemade salami has a wonderful taste to it that only homemade salami can give. It is one of the greatest pleasures, an almost reverent, religious feel to it. Try and make your own, you will never buy shop bought salami again.

Salami

Ingredients

3 kilos of organic shoulder of pork, very coarsely minced (to make two different types of salami)

Curing salt at 28 grams per kilo of meat

250-300 grams of hard back fat of pork

Two tablespoons full of whole black pepper corns

Two tablespoons full of fennel seed

Two glasses of red wine

Two table spoons of dried chilli flakes

Two tablespoons of very good quality paprika

Natural hog runner (sausage casings)

Starter culture (optional)

Method

Before we start I need to say that there are many people who successfully (my father included) make salami with just normal cooking salt, and no starter culture or curing salt. In fact most homemade salami in Italy is made this way and has been for generations. I know that we all want to use natural ingredients, but would strongly advise the use of Curing salt. Curing salt has nitrate and nitrite mixed safely into the salt, it should kill any bad bacteria, and the starter culture is added to colonize the meat with good natural bacteria so that the bad bacteria cannot survive. I use curing salt and starter culture as I believe it gives a better and safer product. Botulism is very rare, but I would not risk it. So the choice is yours. You can buy curing salts and starters online from reputable sellers, I use www.weschenfelder.co.uk they are happy to give advice over the phone.

It is important to remember to keep everything as clean and cold as possible. You will need a large mixing bowl, a sausage stuffing attachment that will fit on to a mincing machine or a hand stuffer. You will also need a stitching needle which you can sterilize over a flame and natural twine.

Place the back fat into the freezer for twenty min to harden. Place the hog runners in water to soak. Remove back fat from freezer and chop into small 5-8mm cubes. In a large bowl add the pork mince and the chopped back fat. Then to the bowl also add 84 grams of curing salt, and the starter culture prepared as per instruction on pack, and then add the wine. It is very important that all the ingredients in the bowl are now well mixed together using your very clean hands. When well combined remove half the contents of the bowl and place in in the fridge while you make the first batch of salami. For the first batch we will make the mild fennel salami. To the bowl add two tablespoons full of fennel seeds and one full of pepper corns. Mix everything together and load the mixture in to your stuffer, take the hog casing and cut off about a metre and a half, tie a knot at one end with the twine, roll the hog skin onto the stuffer (try not to laugh as memories come flooding back) before starting to stuff the casing, prick some holes with the needle into the end of the casing where it is tied. Then, depending on your stuffer, crank by hand or switch on. Fill the casing slowly, this takes practice but fill it firmly and slowly, use the needle to ensure that there are no air pockets. When you have a Salami that is about 8-10 inch long tie it off leave some twine on a loop to hang it from, continue in this fashion till all the mixture is used up. Then we are ready to make the second batch of salami, to the remaining mixture, add all the remaining ingredients and combine well together, and then proceed as with the first batch.

When all your salamis are made, weigh them and record the weight and date, then hang them somewhere warm 18-20C for 24 hours. This will allow the Salami to ripen, and the good bacteria inside the salami to colonize the meat. You will then need to hang the salami somewhere cool (a shed with a window cracked open). You can now if you wish grow that white bacteria that you see growing on Salami in good quality delicatessens. To do this, buy a small amount of that Salami in the delicatessen and with a brush, brush the bacteria off the salami you have brought over your own salami. In a few weeks your salami will be coated with the same bacteria. You will now have to wait for about 4-6 weeks, they should off loss about 1/3 of their weight and firm to the touch. They should now be ready to eat; they will keep for months in the fridge, or vacuum pack them.

Prosciutto Crudo

Air dried ham (Parma style ham)

We are all familiar with Parma Ham. In Italy it is known as Prosciutto Crudo as is all air dried ham outside of the Parma designation area. Parma is unarguably the best you can buy, but there are other air dried hams made all over the south of Italy which are homemade and have a much more rustic flavour.

You can make your own air dried ham, but again you should use proper curing salts. This new method has been used for many years successfully, and gives a more reliable result than the traditional way of placing the meat into a large container of salt. Before trying a whole leg of pork, I would strongly suggest using smaller joints, i.e. loin.

Ingredients

Organic or free range pork loin

Curing salt

Juniper berries

Sweet paprika

Cracked black pepper corns

Method

You can only really make this ham in the colder months of the year; I would recommend starting at the tail end of October, and no later than the end of December

Please follow the instructions for weight of salt to meat exactly as instructed from the supplier of curing salt. Mix a handful of the juniper berries with half the required curing salt and rub well into the meat and the skin so that no part is missed. Wrap the meat tightly in cling film or place in a vac lock bag. Place the joint into a plastic container and place a non-metallic weight on top of the meat, place the container into the fridge for 10-15 days depending on the weight of the meat. At the end of this period, remove from the fridge, unwrap the meat and re-rub with the remaining curing salt. Re-warp and place back into the fridge for a further 10-15 days. At the end of this second period, remove from the fridge and unwrap the meat. Place the meat into a water bath for 10-15 minutes. Remove from the bath and pat dry. At this stage rub the sweet paprika all over the exposed meat but not on the skin. Tie the joint up with some twine with a loop and hang in a warm place (airing cupboard) for 3 days.

Now comes the time for patience, take the meat from the warm area and wrap loosely in muslin cloth and ensure that it is tied at the top and bottom so no flies can get to the meat. Now hang the meat in an unheated shed with a window cracked open so that there is a flow of air. The joint should be ready after when the joint has lost 35% of its weight. It should be slightly firm when pressed. Cut as thinly as possible when needed, and serve.

You can buy curing salt from http://www.sausagemaking.org as a ready to use pack.

Porchetta

Roast belly of pork

What can I say about this wonderful succulent dish? The very essence of Italian style roasted pork. It can be eaten hot or cold between slices of crusty bread. The main flavour is fennel which really makes this roast so special. This recipe will feed a whole party!

Ingredients

2 kilos of boneless belly of pork

1 tablespoon of fennel seeds

Sage leaves

Thyme

Salt and black pepper to taste

3 garlic cloves

Method

Place the belly on to a board skin side down and rub the salt and pepper in well. Place the belly into the fridge while you prepare the fennel seeds. Take a heavy bottomed frying pan and place on a gentle heat, add the fennel seeds to the pan and toast the seed very gently but do not burn. Remove the fennel seeds from the pan and place into a pestle and mortar and grind. Turn on the oven to 220 C, remove the belly from the fridge and rub the ground fennel into the belly, chop up about three or four sage leaves and a sprig of rosemary and sprinkle over the belly. Then add about a three teaspoons of thyme leaves all over the belly. Now roll the belly up tightly and tie with twine. Place the joint onto a roasting tray with 2-3 tablespoons of olive oil and place in the oven for about 20-25 mins. Remove the joint from the oven and cover with foil lower the temp of the oven to 150C and replace the joint to the oven and roast for about 3 hours, this should result is a tender succulent joint. Remove from the oven and place the joint on a warm surface to rest. If eating the joint hot place a couple of ladles of water into the water into the baking tray and over a gentle heat scrape up the bottom of the tray for all the cooking flavours. Carve the joint into thin slices and pour the juices of the pan over the slices and serve. This goes well with a vegetable salad of fresh green beans.

Dolce

Struffoli alla calabrese

Calabrian doughnuts

When I was a young boy, one of the treats of Christmas was Calabrian doughnuts! My mum would fry them up while I waited impatiently at her side to eat them. You need to make bread dough similar to the Pizza dough described in this booklet.

Ingredients

½ kilo of Pizza type dough as in this book but without semolina

Grated lemon zest

Grated orange zest

Honey

Castor sugar (optional)

Method

Make the dough for pizza as described in this book minus the semolina flour. When the dough has risen knock back down again and start to shape the doughnuts. Take a piece of dough about the size of a large egg and form into a circle with a hole in it, so it forms a ring doughnut shape. Once you have made the rings leave them to rest and rise on a floured surface with some oiled cling film to cover them. When the rings of dough are well risen, lift then carefully into medium hot oil cook a few at a time until golden brown. Remove from the oil and drain. Brush with honey, sprinkle on the zests, and roll in caster sugar, if you want to.

Simifreddo

Homemade ice-cream

Ingredients

4 egg yolks

1 whole egg

300 grams of honey

250-300mls of double cream

Method

This Simifreddo is not really ice cream in the true sense of the word, it is not churned and no custard needs to be made. But it tastes as good as ice-cream and it does not need any churning.

Place a large saucepan of water onto boil. In a bowl which will sit over the saucepan add the egg yolks, the whole egg, and the honey. Place the bowl over the pan and turn the heat down to a simmer. Whisk the eggs with an electric whisk or a hand whisk. You will need to whisk over the heat until the eggs and the honey increase in volume and thicken so that the contents of the bowl when lifted and dropped with a spoon will 'plop' back into the bowl. Place bowl to one side. In a separate bowl whisk the cream until it forms soft peaks.

Now gently fold the whisked eggs and honey into the cream, when well combined spoon gently into a container lined with cling film and place into the freezer for at least 2.5 hours. About 15 minutes before serving turn out onto a serving dish and drizzle with some honey. Serve with small almond biscuits.

There are many variations to this, at the stage were you combine the eggs and the cream, you can add espresso coffee, or you can scrape out the contents of a couple of passion fruit, or puree some strawberries into it. The choice is endless, have fun.

Pears with red wine

My Calabrian aunt once cooked this when they had a glut of pears; you can make the same dish by swapping out the pears for peaches.

Ingredients for 4

1 pear per person

Vanilla pod

Or vanilla paste

2 glasses of red wine

Sugar to taste

Method

Peel and cut the pears in half and with a teaspoon hull out the core.

Put the peaches into a pan, add the red wine, and place to one side. Take the vanilla pod and cut open and scrape into the pan with the pears and the wine, (or add a teaspoon of vanilla paste) add two heaped tablespoons of sugar and place on the heat, bring to the boil and then simmer until the pears are soft. Remove the pears and place to one side keeping warm. Continue to cook down the wine until it is syrup. Pour over the pears and serve.

Torrone

Nougat

This nougat is always welcome at Christmas or Easter; it gives more than just a nod to the historic Arabic influence in Calabria andSouthern Italy. It uses only three main ingredients of honey, almonds, and egg whites. You can if you want add some orange and lemon peel or candied peel, you don't need to but I think it makes it much nicer.

I have to say that it is also a bit time consuming to make, but on a wet cold Sunday it will bring some much needed sunshine into your kitchen.

Ingredients

Rice paper for lining

3 egg whites or two large egg whites

350 grams of honey

150-200 grams of peeled whole almonds

Orange and lemon peel or candied peel (optional)

Method

Line the bottom of a small square baking tin with the rice paper.

Place the almond in a baking tray and place in the oven at 180 C and bake until slightly toasted, remove from oven and place to one side to cool.

Take a large pan and fill around a quarter with water. Next get a deepish dish that will sit on top of the pan without touching the water and act as a Bain Marie.

Pour the honey into the Bain Marie dish and place over a low heat. At the same time whip the egg white into stiff peaks. When the honey has melted add the egg white and stir constantly but slowly for 45-55mins. The mixture will slowly begin to thicken and at this stage add the almonds and peel and you will notice that it will suddenly thicken even more. Continue to stir through this stage and keep stirring for a further 30-40 minutes. By this time the mixture should be very stiff. Take a drop of the mixture and drop into cold water and it should stay together in a soft jelly state. You can now pour the mixture into the prepared baking tin. Then press a top layer of rice paper onto the mixture and smooth out by pressing firmly all over. Place in a cool place and when fully cooled remove from the tray and cut with a heavy knife into one inch squares.

Made in the USA
Middletown, DE
11 March 2016